viewpoints

barbara bulova brown

To John, family, friends and teachers

viewpoints
Barbara Bulova Brown

Published by The Cheshire Press
An imprint of The Cheshire Group
Andover, MA 01810

ISBN: 978-0-9960210-8-1
Library of Congress Control Number: 2017939206

Printed in the United States of America

Brown, Barbara Bulova

viewpoints

CONTENTS

I

STORM

Storm

Once it was August and we were young.
On the lake, small isles spiny with dark pines
Punctuated the blue on blue horizon,
Usurping views of oncoming weather.
Well-used water skis stowed in the stern,
Now movements, postures and conversation
Became languid as the air,
Opulent with warmth and color.

In an instant, as if the filmmaker
Had selected black and white to make his point
Or reverse the course of time,
The scene was changed to gray.
Our erstwhile navigator, suddenly frantic,
Raced his fruitless race with fate
While a crisp world-wide wall of rain
Marched toward us.

We, watching the sheet's approach
Accompanied by ominous rumbling
And sweet ripples then where waters met,
Were armed with electric, humid air,
All ambiguous before the true assault.
Then wholly drenched, we felt the storm
Pass around and through, endless moments,
Minutes we never would forget.

There was now no seeing,
Each alone as we truly were,
Facing overwhelming forces always there.
Our proud boat became mere board,
Our skin, thinnest of membranes.
Suspended so, we could only pray

That there would be no lightning,
Please, to fry us wetly in our places.

Swiftly and at last, the curtain showed
Its other side, receded as it had come.
Behind it and all innocence,
The sky, now gentle and storm free,
Brought back a freshened day.
Color and volition returned to our lives,
Such as they were and were to be,
Full but feeble in comparison.

Short Journey

Bars of spikes and loops,
A fence of strong black iron,
Kept me in one long summer,
Kept me lonely and alone,
Standing, seeing, holding on.

Older kids at times stopped by
On their way to older things,
Stopped to tease, to scare,
This little girl standing there,
Teaching me, at five, by that gate,
The ways of spider and of snake.

One day, two of dad's patients stopped
To take me for a skip-filled walk
For ice cream a mere short block
Away; that innocent vanilla cone
Was smooth and cool to tongue and throat.

Back again and still obedient,
I was quickly sent up to my room
With its dolls and fatly floral walls,
Confused, ashamed, confined anew
For all that hot and sunny day,
Taunted by a window view.

In that time of its worst season
For polio there was no defense,
A fact I did not, could not have known.
Years later when I asked the reason,
I learned the truth of that lonely season.

Mosquito

I'm angry to be shut inside today,
With little choice against the vast array.
My skin is mottled with feeding sites,
Various, calamined, hilly bites.

My favorite riddle is at its expense,
Knock-knock in level though more picturesque.
Why can't the mosquito fly through the screen door?
I ask, smirking with prescience at the fore.

The only answer— as it buzzes at my portal,
No menace now, especially when made mortal,
Flying there in its frenzied zag and zig—
Is entirely obvious: its sneakers are too big!

Thus to its stems, fragile in extreme,
Built to 'light on us unfelt and unseen,
Upon them I've conferred **my** sneakers and **my** feet,
Implying mean intent as well as comic pique.

I've burdened the insect with my ungainliness,
My emotions and my selfishness,
Forgetting, in vengeful joke about its urgent need,
That **we** murder those on whom we feed.

Companion

My tulips as yet unopened
Were disappearing two by two,
Likely in early evening.
I rushed to buy the cure

Called Companion, which
When I pressed, sprayed
Onto my hand and on the heads
I was trying to protect.

Last night two more tulips went:
Reds were first, then the yellows.
Good for three months,
Companion's label promised.

The next day, I found,
Stretched out nearby
And more than asleep,
The victim and likely culprit.

I returned the can:
I had not meant to trade
A squirrel for my flowers, I said.
That little death is on my head.

Weather

In darkening day, rain dashes plans;
Petals that cannot stay become confetti
To gather in pointless confusion
Before being blown away.

Louder, louder, the roof rattles.
In sunny Sarajevo yet more snipers
Riddle victims with their random sprays;
Bullets and bombs reap rooms of shrouds.

The inconvenient rain hinders us.
We change our plans, perhaps light a fire,
Make cake or love, all before dinner.
Someday soon it may be sunny here.

Winter for Two Geminis

Married during a February blizzard
We formed a storm-restricted party.
Front door stayed open; I was last to go,
Shoes bleeding blue into the snow.

For our first official Christmas
I gave you a sleek black case,
An upgrade of your battered brown
For future travels from our town.

Arguing, many years on, you said
You'd leave, suitcase ready, packed.
I threw it out our bedroom window,
Later to retrieve it from the snow.

Your gift had been a sturdy sander
To fix the home to which I was wed.
Now, chasing memories of our youth,
I wonder, 'meant to wear me smooth?

Dishwashing

From back to front,
Dirty dishes I neatly place.
You do the opposite,
Saying they need space.

I sigh, at least
They're out of sight,
And of course later
Replace them right.

In a marriage of
Different temperaments,
Details like this
Must lend some sense.

To Bloom in Autumn

In long enduring marriages
Partners come to intertwine,
Like clematis in the garden,
Bountiful sturdy vine.

With roots long since transplanted,
Each must seek some room,
Or like that social climber,
Will find it cannot bloom.

Browns at Home

Gray brown, our clapboards look best
At twilight when they complement
A surrounding evanescent scene.

Grass, green-patched in contrast
To shades of autumn's rust,
Holds on, alive, but likely just.

We two wear skins in spotted brown
And once brown hair gone gray and white,
Wintry versions of lawn's summer blight.

Now through home's repeated painting,
And time and energy more dear,
Gray brown's subtle beauty becomes clear.

Plans

After your separation from your wife,
Apparently women flocked to you,
Women of different ages, heights
And such. You even went on a date
The same Halloween night we met,
Though she complained about
Your cheeriness as well as being late.

Years later, married happily,
We agreed it could be so for you again;
You should not be alone— no judgment
There from me, if that next mate
Were younger and prettier than I,
Of course a curvy blonde—
As long as you could laugh again.

She would be spouse number three,
Not my two as you'd remind
Me in your teasing way.
That's what could have been
If it were I who sleeps the sleep
That's after life and not, sadly,
As it happened, you.

II

NATURE

Nature

Rains come drop by drop
On late snow, pounding down,
So that below, the cellar,
Though carved from rock,
Hosts a rolling tide.

This has occurred before
And is thus better in a way
Than it would have been
Before pump and pipe
And cemented trough repair.

I built many barriers,
Did my best, I tell myself,
Working now with plumbers' putty
To mark and fill where bubbles
Show persistent gaps.

Even the sturdiest of walls
Cannot resist time's step.
Still, and yet again, I try
To seal these many markers
When nearly dry of cloudy tears.

Such vigilance, I think,
At least builds character,
As the familiar and dear wear away,
Exposing in us and for us
What in life we all must lose.

Intimations

It seems there is
Too much of nature:
Late June's searing rain
Darkens earth, soaks the spirit.
You liked this weather once
When your walk was steady.

Now our ailing cat sleeps
More too. Gentle-seeming,
She eats parts of her gift
Of large new-killed rabbit,
Its severed halves marked
By a deep red organ bulb.

I inter the rabbit's carcass
With gloved hands, the same
That cemented cellar holes
Where fetid water waited
And mold would bloom,
Like that on this summer's roses.

This year lilies open early,
Ruddy red, peach and lemon,
Urged to too ripe fullness
By steamy rebel sunlight,
Mottled isles in seas of showers,
Teased as we are for another day.

Fall Cleaning

Our house is lighter
As we shed the weight
Of limitlessness.

Dusty worn rugs hurled
From above bump and slide
To oblivion.

Beside our driveway
Stands a mute totem pole
Of our old TVs.

Yet I buy bright bowls
For winter's soup: a promise
That we hope to keep.

Winter Preparation

Adjust the choke, gently;
The machine is old; allowances
Must be made. Pump the button,
Turn the key, then pull the cord
Straight and rapidly.

The throaty roar is full,
Deafening in the wintry air.
Readjust the choke and push
Slowly: a new white cloud
Arcs to settle on each hill.

You set me to practice,
This task I think the only one
I surely would not want.
There is much to do
For now and just in case.

Transition

I totter about, my steps limited and small;
Years it seems, yet it's only been since fall.
Our lives are changing and I'm resenting
The unmannered spark of each awakening.

This morning greets me in one sense full;
It is more than dream, the silent pull
Of last night's baking, this nasal spurring
To first footfall and cold de-bedding.

Dreams of caring deeds come unpowered
By my side-lived seconds upon hours.
Others' dramas grant me needed sleep,
While our hope must wait, seeded deep.

I Worry

Nights I worry
Especially when I hear
Your discordant lung music
Of familiar phlegmy hacks,
And you're still smoking.

I'm not ready, never was,
To say goodbye, and already miss
Your snoring warmth beside me,
My playful pokes that turn you over,
The humor and the history.

You finally told me that April night
When they'd uncovered your disease,
Of your first-born's final day.
Decembers still you've had to treat
With more than darkened rooms.

Now we disregard mere crankiness;
This chronic fear is something else.
Yet you still voice contentment
In living your own hours.

Our dance now is no metered thing
But a dirge with its molasses moves.
A stopped clock correct twice a day
Outstrips this dubious synchronicity.

Yet I wake with some optimism
Each morning when the day is new.
The arising's ever more difficult,
Like your days, these days.
I worry about you.

Imperatives

We talk of your body
As if it were public territory
Where cells still yours but foreign
Wage oxymoronic civil war.

Experts are bombing
And the effect on the masses
Silent? Deadly?
Is hard to fathom.

We want it clear-cut
But causes are complex
And of long standing;
Opportunities have been seized.

In your body it is clear
Which came first, whose rights,
But force too decimates,
Can create a "saved" My Lai.

To watch you, hear your groans,
I and those who know much more,
Hope to remain steady,
Try to mitigate your pain.

Personified

From out of the deepest shadows it came
Menacing jaws and teeth dripping gore
Eyes of yellow fire annihilating all
Hatred spewing from every pore

Moving back and forth
All-seeing
It stares us down
Daring us to move

My sleeping lips twitch in sympathetic baring
My jaw clenches unrelenting
Fists tighten and teeth gnash
Anxiously defiantly

I see it still
Though I think I am now awake
Waiting   then standing
Horrified and expectant

Waiting for the Doctor

In the story of a train bound for hell, a man
Bargains with the devil. He's handed a watch
He can stop to freeze time, but the man
Wants to know, as time speeds to his end,
Whom will he bed? Wed? Father? And so on.

He thwarts the devil on the final train.
Back here a pale wraith arrives, wheels
Clacking under her; has she any will or say?
Here a breathless man coughs his words;
In-tubed bodies sit for countless hours.

Those with health can play, adjust their stances,
Gauge the weather, opponents' strength;
Otherwise they might give in too soon. Patience
Is not a given in our fast-paced world. I sit and wait
With our mates, watching heroes endure.

(Please)

Nike advises, *(just) do it,*
But it is not in this sense
That I bark it out,
An exercise like others
I think unlikely to be of aid.

She starts again:
She has to call,
He's not on the list.
See, not there:
For an EKG she needs to call.

So do it, I say, my arms
Lifting as I turn away
And swiftly walk to where
My husband waits
In his wheelchair.

In the Hospital

Your cane upended on the chair
When I arrive you aren't there

Moans of pain echo from a door
Pungent cleaner slicks the floor
My *March of Folly* goes unread
Nurses work to change your bed

Toothpicks batteries a hat
Your list for me and more than that
Family members to make aware
Of this second time you are there

Still you seek cause and effect
While doctors prime you to protect
You beyond the newest claims to space
Where rampant cells rush the pace

Now tests have made it all too plain
Time to defend your spine, your brain

More

More time please
I ask
A time I will not take for granted,
Not this time

A time to rest
To regain strength
A time
This time to temper anger

I want more time
So you once again
Can lift one full cup
Or just this fluffy towel

Last Prelude and Feud

Tired of that room, the rooms, of visiting
Or merely viewing, the endless sadness
Of trying, needing to write of it, and oh,
The letting go, so precious,
Each piece, so slow, but some relief
At times when charts look better
Or when I could mourn alone.

Long ago we chose, though moves
Were mostly yours at first;
That picture of you in your 30's comes,
Handsome, wise and mature.
Now there's this you lying there,
Less shaved than you like,
Less, less and less.

You are in the hospital again,
Pointing to newspaper ads.
You ask which, unable to check
An address book nor recall
Our lawyer's name. I feign ignorance,
But you threaten to call him anyway
For a separation.

I think this not so much from me
But from that room where you're confined
And in which you're likely thinking—
In as much as your beleaguered brain
Can generate something clear
Though with the will that drives you—
That maybe you will never leave.

Soon after, before that numbered door,
I receive a final diagnosis:

Secondary tumors are growing
In your lungs, likely from continued smoking.
The doctors told me, no, you should
Remain here: your lungs will fill again.
All hope I had was gone.

This time when I went in you did not ask
But somehow you must have known.
We did the most to keep my promise,
Obtained a special bed, a nurse and hospice:
That communicated what I could not.
Your family was there for that last week.
I knew you wanted to come home.

What You Wanted

Did you want another chart,
Its jagged lines of blood counts
Marching up and down to mark
Your life in its final paces,

Another attempt to tame
Wild figures, one so low that visits
Could only be as aliens
Garbed in glove, mask and gown?

Your lovely muscled legs
That bore you six miles every
Early morning were slack
And worse than weightless.

Even home your baleful look
Perhaps I misunderstood as when
I woke to see your upraised fist
Which I took to be your will,

And asked, *You're fighting still?*
But you were past speech.
On I went, gave permission.
Your eyes widened then.

I said, *When you're ready,
It's all right to go.*
No one can tell you
How hard it is, those last words,

Their timing and presumption,
Those last touches,
Those looks,
Those last farewells.

Questions

Was it a time for men together
When we ministering three,
A nurse, one daughter and a wife,
Sat quietly beyond the door
While you worked at dying
That night to early morning?

I know I promised always to be
With you and gave you leave to go,
The hardest words to ever utter,
And summoned family for that week.
You rallied despite the bed you hated.
Was it better with all of us at home?

Late Tuesday night your grown sons
Told their stories to your barely
Conscious form. I entered briefly,
Heard your breath so hoarse
And labored, saw your body's struggles.
I wondered then, where were you?

The nurse and I walked outside
In the silent cooling dark, to ease
A sudden nausea and buoy
My ebbing strength. We returned
To a different scene, where all
But you were gathered.

Can certain courses not be changed?
I realized once again that in this life
At least, there can be no returning.
Yet that morning a gray-brown
Bird perched on the fence and stayed,
Despite my madly flapping arms.

Necessity

Leaning out the window
Watering geraniums,
I felt brackets loosen
And heavily give way:
Thus from my helpless hand
The whole box hung.

Far past cursing, I thought
Of you working, requesting
A tool when you were fine.
Now decision mine, I acted
Quickly, lifting liner and all
To let it fall, twenty feet or so.

This I did with faint remorse,
And, in fact, with satisfaction
In the smash; without recourse
And too fast for second thought,
I had to act. I know that for me
To carry on it's necessary to let go.

III

DOORS

Doors

A dream of a door unhinged
Came pleasantly:
I could re-attach
And use it for a life.

Leaving it,
Walking through,
My son asked later,
Did you consider that?

Did I say *I love you,*
Especially at the end?
Whisper, *I'll miss you,*
Hoping you could hear?

We shared a life
For half of mine,
But not a death.
Your door was different.

Afterwards

It must have rained last night,
Slightly wet the desert earth
And sent an ant to mount my arm.
Sudden is its slapped demise.

The house is still, arranged,
So this outrage isn't right,
A parody of my ancient
Bring the outside in desire.

Challenge lurks here, everywhere
In this nearly empty house,
Unaccustomed to such daylight
And a wife so uneven.

Replacing

Today I moved so many things
Mostly different than yesterday's:

Some went inches, others floors,
And likely more retraced their paths.

I know I've said things aren't important
And some days wish for a few rocks only

To sit by walls on roughened floors,
But know that I would move them too

And exchange them, turn them, endlessly.
It's hard, you know, to let things be.

We Differed

You closed off northern windows,
Pulled down shades. I acquiesced,
Though by nature, I've always gazed
Through windowed patterns at azure hills

And at the vastness of the changing sky,
Which you in workplace formulae
Used to predict what atmospheres
To counteract for missiles to survive.

Your notebooks idle dense on shelves,
Cold without your ken. What irony
That heat transfer was your chosen field,
When your body's heat you couldn't summon.

You pulled down shades that I would raise;
Your concern was loss of heat.
I think for me it was mostly sight,
As in dullness now I crave the light.

TV Hours

In flickering blues and purples
The bloodless counts of hours
Hold thoughts suspended
Though some escape
To skim books and magazines
In attempts at reading

Intersecting plots at best
Gravely play off minor meanings
He cheats or she
They joke or try or should
They make a table
Buy and fix a house
Three rooms done in half an hour
Love and death in double that

Camera so close
The eye perceives the stitch
Or watches for a pulse
There is no room for worry
In this wintry recipe
With its few pinches of sanity

My eyes are open
Waking to another day
Hardly awake these hours
I live a lying life
Couched here in the living room

Widows' House

This house you found that we loved
shows its darker side
(to her and then to me);

this home we made, you and I kept
and fixed and cleaned
(for us and family),

this place which her husband left
to take a bird-stopped flight
(and die instantly),

this house of wood where you retired
and then were brought
(to remain in part),

is ruled by a kitchen, a warm room,
where she, then I finally
(she with bottle),

sat and sit doing what women do,
living our little lives
(conserving fuel).

Housewifery

After every visitor I find
I clean and make small changes
Seeing the house through their eyes
More clearly than otherwise

I did such chores and more
For you when you were sick
For you new-planted roses bloomed
Trees I trimmed and stone steps groomed

Already there's much you haven't seen
Each purchase and each change
So from a clear point on they're new
To me and through me you

Name

The inchoate before a name
Has a power more than human,
This largest of an unknown—
Chaotic, no, greater still,
Past any asymptote,
A naming of the unnamable:

Is that now where you are?
I think I worried needlessly,
Dealt with ashes—you didn't care—
But in my night you appeared
At last, a first, and I aware of you
There, gently, firmly, holding me.

Do you have a name now?
Strange, I rarely called you John
But Honey and Dear, my names
For you even when we'd argued.
You marked our dates, monitored
Things and made me Woman.

Now your name must be spirit
If your belief can make it so.
Yet I wonder if a part awaited
Your eighth grandchild's recent birth,
Re-earthed and mild with Down's,
A different John named Nathan.

On Thought and Time

The tunnel of light at life's end
Is explained as myriads of neurons
Firing heavily in the brain's core.

Time itself is believed to speed or slow
When increased focus or some crisis
Changes the ratio of event to time.

Four anxious months seem as one,
With no like marker since your death,
And Christmas arrives the day after August.

Enter Henry to Fill the House

Good dog, Henry,
I say,

Not because you upchucked
On the rug, but
That you stayed put
While I cleaned up.

Henry and I get Lessons

Good dog it seems
Is not enough;
We both work hard
To reach *OK*, meaning
Done, and when released,
Merely good enough.

Then comes *off*,
Not at all the same
As *down*, which
Puts you flat
After years of
Springing from a *sit*.

Now, *wait* does not
Mean *stay*; no,
S*tay* means freeze,
Which seems a game
But is actually quite serious.

Leave it says don't touch,
Even with your tongue.
I hope I'm learning to relax,
Yet to quickly tug your leash
For mutual attention.

All this must become reflex
For us, with you at five
And I considerably more.
Now I finally at least and last,
Must admit, *who knew*?

Here

Late morning sky lightens toward reflection,
Clouds above and below so clear that if I did not know
Which came first I could reside in each,
No thought of air as cold as space nor lake
As smothering in its languid liquid weight.

My weight and years not always gain,
I live in this now, this spring when life begins,
When wind and age peel bark to bare new skin,
Even as advancing branches creak.

Wind rustles paper too, a place where writings bloom,
Stirs all life, ripples surface, wilds the animal within.
This wind is I, and sun, and brown pine-needled path,
On which tracks and marks my panting dog,
Tongue lolling from his open smile.

Dog's hind legs fling back earth:
He leaves his padded scent.

Gone

I am thrown back into life with hope
Yet my dream door lies off its hinges
As my thoughts dwell on the maintenance
And expanse that is our house.

I know you're not coming back,
And yet, and yet… I see
These are my days of "otherwise"
That follow my half life of married being.

My ginger dog matches walls; my new car,
The clapboards. You shared neither,
Like my parents, who'd have beheld with joy
The bold adults our two now are.

This I have so often thought,
Though they are not a single year
Like you but a full two decades
Gone, away from all that's here.

Changing

Changing my ring from left hand
To right, I become new unmarried.
This symbol of our weakened tie
Resides in a simple band of gold
That time will never tarnish.

This year's taxes are on my desk;
I tackle them in draft mode first.
It's been seven months now
Or more precisely nearly eight—
Odd that the even have more weight.

Deceased I write for you in pencil;
In one month and ink it is official.

After Ten Days Away

My skin crawls, its minor mutinies affecting hours,
Though this armor still defends in faithful flexibility
After more than three score years.

When I wake I check evidence of poison ivy
Unseen in English garden treks, in its march on me
Most intense in newest spots.

Here summer yields a swamp-green pool, my closet
Smacks of dissonance, and my usual food is bland;
Winds coolly trumpet season's end.

Beginning Spanish- Gracias para Ud. Sra Ana

Roll all those r's, especially dos in a row.
Have fun, tongue, learning this nuevo lingo.
Forget the drifting, whining diphthongs,
For they're unromantic American things.
En espanol, vowels are singular and heard,
Rushing precisely away, from and toward

The clicking of their quick consonants.
Hay siempre mas cosas para practicar:
Verbos, detailes y endless preguntas,
Que, como se dice, go in- and outwards,
Questions to elicit those algunas veces,
Funny, hardworking beginner phrases.

Take care with your words: some palabras
Are tricky, like pollo or hambre—such as
Prior to tener—to say what really you want.
Beware those cognates that actually aren't,
Like coma—a possible cure for the faint—
Or embarazada that in French is enceinte.

Ahora, now, bears an insider pause; while down
You are slowed, you can admire its sound.
A pillow melodious is the flowing almohada,
Onto which you can sink your cabeza cansada.
To gossip sounds wrong, but chismear, dear,
Is an amorous invitation, at least to the ear.

Then listen to nueve, y huevo, llaves—these
Seem far from English's nine, and egg, keys,
Which said together become x in Spanish.
Thus we arrive, after y, at zeta—tres dashes,
An end, though we hope not of our learning.
Perhaps, quizas, it's, muy bien, a beginning.

Trip Report: Ten Days at the End of my Daughter's Nine Month Honeymoon Abroad

When in Rome or this case Madrid
Watch your luggage as I should have did
In teams they were and I was lucky
Having not much for picky plucky

Thus begins my trippy whinge
A special Spanish my revenge
Said I who knows what and often fast
That puzzles some who laugh at last

For Calle Major I questioned Calle Meillor
Or Better Street which none could answer
Tres from my mouth once came out treinta
At least just mumbled to the waita

To save time and ticket we chose to climb
Left on steep stairs by lift behind
Though many places were cerrado closed
To much culture we were exposed

Timing I admit was not the best
Our war in Iraq began day I left
For Spain though it declared itself allied
Polls and nightly protests that belied

The eve of my return all of Europe
Advanced time an hour making a dope
Of each who went like me to airport clueless
Thus that day we mostly flew less

'can't complain though here I tried
Good food and wine even churros fried
Three cities historic two hostels clean
The newlyweds looking after me

Renewed after resting for one week
Too seriously about trips I cannot speak
For quiet it is here and not as vital
'nothing like travel for feeling extra-societal

Checkup

The doctor concludes his annual
Inspection of my ocular acuity:
No further deterioration of eyes or skin.
As ever meticulous, he persists,
So why were you taking medication?

My countenance parked in neutral,
I do not speak. Anxiety? he prompts,
Gazing into my pupil-distended eyes.

Well, I start, taking bait and diving in,
My husband's been gone almost four
Years; I wave dismissively, as if
This moment, at least, could be erased.

I'm sorry, he says, while gathering
Essentials for his next patient.

I continue, and I think this age is hard
For many women, houses emptying,
The hormonal—but he and nurse are
At the door, so I add thank you, much as
I had politely said perdon to pickpockets
Blocking my way off the metro in Madrid.

IV

MOVING

Moving: The Closing

Lessening, letting go—these lessons
Are mine in this business deal
A closing mainly for the buyers
To make their purchase final, real
The house to do with what they will

As did we—they do not know nor care
About removed windows, button switches
They see inlaid floors and see refinish
Certain walls and see need removal
Appliances and see not stainless steel

Fixer upper, not as nice as what they left
They say in my, the seller's, presence
Whose emotions are not lessened
Ties not broken as I had thought
Perhaps I should not have left

Whereas my lawyer should, he said,
Follow this deal through to its end
I suspect his motive one of currency
To him my broker talks of trends
Likes statistics, bends them well

Their broker-friend tap taps on
Her laptop and says little, mouth
Smiling at buyers who sign and sign
Wife sharp with vexation at the time
Glares at us on the other side

Their lawyer heads the table
Quite handsome in his office
Deals out and collects all paper
Disburses checks from his account
Seller learns and may know better

Later, but this night, bereft of sleep
Reads as diversion from unease
Once owner, seller, and now outsider
I am dispossessed though by intention
And reckon this, likely later, a good thing

Flip Side: What I Expected

They sit down at the long table amicably,
The buyers and sellers—that is, we,
Becoming friends in the exchange of property,
That proceeds quickly and oh so smoothly.

Signing all papers with a flourish and smile,
Buyers are grateful for a house with such style
And glad to have gotten a genuine steal,
While seller too is content with the deal.

All parties collaborate fully;
Brokers and lawyers each do his duty;
Buyers thank seller for the neat job in leaving,
The presents she left and her incredible speed.

Even after two weeks packing up 34 years
And moving to a new home that did pass inspection,
Such an easy, clean process this could have been:
But not tempting enough to do it again.

New Address

Here I have a new address.
For this modern house of one,
And like my surname when we wed,
Changed faster than I could fathom.

Your face still flickers
In different ways and lasts
Through album years of photos
With aspects I still seem to know,
Until that final startling mask.

At times I feel your touch, or hear
Your laugh, a cough, your sigh.
I see our history both in mind
And in simple objects left behind.

Why now and from where
Come these awakenings,
That in smallest hours I can't avoid?
I receive in aching sleeplessness
A slow and awful clarity.

I Dream of Our Brown House

I saw a slight disheveled man
Clearing snow from a nearby drive
And boldly went to salute him in his work.

Kind in his Clark Kent glasses,
He mentioned someone 82,
Not eighty, too, I was hoping as I nodded,
Knowing I didn't hear all that he had said.

The large house next door contained a room
Now newly bright and open:
Beautiful I thought, and told him so.

He said the house was his, appearing proud
Despite his modest guise; next to us
My old neighbor's fence was still
A wracked and peeling wreck.

Waking then and fully home, I feel
Lighter in my newer space, relieved of that
Old brown house and it as well of me.

Winter Interior

Sun slants through slats and glass.
Who says this light is weak in winter?
What do they know of northern thirst?

Reflections on foliage, chairs and such
Interrupt as myriad brightly angled spots;
Light cascades from a window triptych.

Cement Buddha seems to burst his bounds,
Serenely seated on the hearth, his formal fingers,
Half smile, lowered lids, inward and unknowable.

Rain

Why reflect on what
This pewter sky sheds day on day,
That in back bellies up leaves and branch
And slowly soaks Elsewhere's snow,
Puddling all the Heres and Theres?

Weather outside mirrors mood
Or conversely makes it, mocks it,
Dull yet ominous in its empty gray:
Says no need to leave, to wade in muck;
Reveals challenges that lie within.

Mere contemplation, though, yields
Its peace and pleasure: garden-to-be is there
In mind, while ground yet frozen waits,
And Will Be expects another weather
That is not Now, but dwells in dreams
Of When and How and of a greener Then.

Discovering Wetlands:
ESL Vocabulary Exercise

A cold bright blue day it is, blue on white
For both the sky and *mulish* snow that will
Not melt. In back, stand *intermittent gnarled*
Trees, *obviating* a hilly *strategy* that would
Overwhelm the house in some *absurd* downward
Leap. Instead, *abscesses* surround most trunks
Where there is melt, icy *bayous* mirrored blue
That present themselves as if some giant hand,
Obtuse and *obstinate*, had *holked* them out.

I Think I See

Red fingers reach from sepia toward glass,
    Extending twigs with subtlety,
        Not noticeable just yesterday.
            I think, how could that be?

Before long, in warmer hours,
They will flower, servants
To this season, though
They would not disagree.

Then their sap will course more swiftly
    Beneath hoary rough exteriors,
        Tempting me to paint
            In what I hope is joy,
                To magnify, to simplify

The ridges, grain, lichen,
Lines and whorls of calluses
That live on their rounded,
Sturdy, shaded trunks.

But I romanticize,
    Anthropomorphize,
        For that is what I do
            In often futile longing
                For pattern, order, rule.

V

PORTRAITS

Portrait

She leans on her hand
Doesn't know I'm catching her
With my charcoal stick:
The slant of her head
Angled down and away
Mouth and chin half hidden
And anchored even in sleep

Her wrinkles read subtle
In the soft low light
As with my kneaded eraser
New light is allowed to flow
Across her all-white hair
Down her nose, her cheek
And at the bend of wrist

Quick but right
Drawn before she wakes
In twenty minutes at most
And there she sits:
Nana, fifty years later,
Framed and supported on a ledge
Still asleep

Kurt

Best friends, we agreed he should not date us both,
so we shrewdly chose, which seemed fine
with the kind, tall boy with warm brown eyes,
sensuous mouth, short brown hair and prominent ears.

Kurt and I spoke long afternoons on the phone,
often of baseball; weekends we walked;
dates often included rum and cokes at his house.

We went to his senior prom, and after a night
cruise on Lake George said fond good nights
outside my house until 2:30 in the morning.

Kurt found his father in the garage,
his suicide not quite complete, ensuring
he would never be the same again.

My father, the physician who also cared for his
alcoholic mother, recommended him for college,
and later told me that Kurt was majoring in music.

I saw Kurt once around that time. His eyes were sad.
We did not speak of his mother, again relapsed,
of his father who could no longer speak at all,
nor even of our once-beloved Yankees.

In Remembrance

After our mother's sudden death, she left
The three of us on separate paths, each
Struggling to knit up a life. In that year

Dad was slowly dying in resonance,
Allowing cancer its way within him,
His will to live shattered with this loss.

Later I briefly glimpsed their wartime cards.
A captain in the Europe that they'd fled,
He penned strong words in his artistic hand.

She wrote of me, the infant he'd seen once.
Physician too, she was concise: *Come back
To me soon, my love. Take care of yourself.*

Gift

Poets in the bookstore's café
Read their odes to love,
But where I am, all is wrong,
With journals, calendars, tomes,
And views of cities from above,

As I search for a gift to bring,
Not for your still quick mind
To wrap around, and who knows
What you now can hold; at last
I buy an art book that I find,

Too aware that your only task
Is to free yourself from life,
And the fact that you ask
Us to share in your last days,
Is all and must suffice.

Neil and his Family

Six weeks, Neil scrawls in his notebook of duties, lists,
tasks and deadlines; disgusted and overwhelmed,
he throws it into a corner.

Meanwhile his sister labors to breathe. Skilled
social worker still, Marsha has seen much and
supported many. For herself, she says that she
has few regrets.

It's what she wants that counts, Neil, made responsible,
insists to all. His legal knowledge provides little
comfort, like the food and drink he takes and offers,
irrelevant now to her.

Friends, bidden and not, come to commiserate, support,
wonder, and express opinions. Ultimately they
re-examine their own lives.

Neil orchestrates, to his own surprise, gently and with
humor. His unraveling is gradual and nearly unnoticed
until two weeks later, when a younger cousin challenges
several of his decisions.

Once again, his story differs from Cheryl's and his family's:
he threatens to call the police if she doesn't leave, his push
was only a slap, and he is punished for what he regards
as his integrity, his reaction to their demands.

Within a day he is estranged from everyone, the sole
exception always having been his sister, who has left
them all in her sleep.

Revisiting

Last night a college friend
From years ago came by:
Our dialogue was spare;
Perhaps there was too much
To say or too few words,
Or our time too brief.

As it is with good friends,
It seemed no time had passed,
And she looked unchanged.
We went about our tasks as if still
Apartment-mates, in that space
Between graduate school and life.

She gave me knowing,
Searching looks, and then,
With a new and shining smile,
Said she'd met someone,
Revealing when gently pressed,
His name, Harry Goodman.

An envious happiness for her
Remained, as I awoke remembering:
First that Harry was her father
And secondly that my last visit
With her was five years ago,
A week before her death.

Sestina Tribute

Good bye and hello, they said, these two men
Close to me—they said with arm and legs,
Male limbs mothering, one in bidding only
A farewell, who reached a wasted limb
To nearly touch this thoughtful child,
His grandson, who later would a father be.

Now grandson greets son just come to be,
Bonds him to this growing tribe of men.
The lanky male but recently a child
Holds his day-old son at length on legs
So that the sleeping one covers limbs
From mid-thigh to knee only.

These images link for me, not only
In intensity, one the pain parting must be,
But in the contrast between these limbs.
Yet here the similarity of the men
Is not borne physically, since their legs
Always differed, but lies in loving so a child.

Surprised each man was to see in such a child
Himself, thought, and continuity, not only
Innocence and helplessness. Whether held on legs
Or just beyond a helpless arm, it is not to be
That the child sees a touch. In the minds of men
There is soft language, not just the clash of limbs

Engaged in arts of war and sports, where limbs
Are strong and power leased to each male child.
There is more than this to the world of men.
To the daughter of the shy learned man reaching only
Air—to me, that image of his yearning was to be
Borne as lasting sorrow. Not until my son's legs'

Image did I the outreached arm with these legs
Connect, the support given with careful limbs.
I saw love, pictured generations to be
Born and thus gained serenity. That this child
Could become such a man, for this I only
Can give thanks, and honor all these men,

Father, husband too of rugged legs, our first child.
On family trees, limbs—its children—not only
Bear its stories but what is to be, women and the men.

Boxes

Towards this too we move,
And moved, we two relatives
Are left to sort and shred.

At 93, she left her boxes neat,
And demanded of each she met
The best and often more.

But generous too, though this
At times for gain, she noted
Gifts in thirty books of days.

In these, she listed costs
And even calls, that dwindled
This past year to many days apart.

She kept warranties from half
A century in boxes never random,
Spent years in their revision.

She gave up a country, two houses
And three husbands, and after a final
Fall, desire for any nourishment.

We found three boxes full of gloves,
Seven hotel packs of thread, and
Countless unopened packages.

Lethal pills we flushed away,
Wet and burned boxes, decades
Worth of financial documents.

There were bags of bags and boxes
Of boxes, and in the last, labels
She cut from her medications.

No, in the very last were ashes,
His and hers, committed to earth
In simple ritual as she had wished.

Take Care

In croton country we see
Or hear few of middle age,
So we are young in this place
Of wheeled chairings, puzzle-making
And of repeated leave takings.

At dinner, its portions big and bland,
We hear hints of lives once lived
From familiar oft-planned groups
Hunkered busily at their tables.
Do we intrude on our own future space?

My northern home needs someone
Younger, I think, as I, shrinking, wander
In my own rattling-around capacities.
And what about those who do not choose
To age together as they do?

At home, plants persist and hibernate,
As meanwhile of our wintry cares
We care must take. You'd think
Croton country more care free,
But care must follow those in need.

What Remains

I think of you two
Who must care more than I:
Fine dust is all I specify,
Efficiency in the means;
Then you can scatter me.

Ceremony I leave to you,
To you I entrust my care:
Put me wherever;
Nurturing flowers
I might prefer, or in water.

But be gentle then
With your thoughts,
For I'll remain in these alone,
For a generation or two,
My son and my daughter.

Misled

Awakened by the phone past ten,
By a call not even meant for me:
From a puzzle of a person, she
Spews worried winds of energy.

She'd said she follows one who speaks
Of following too often those she meets;
Then sold, in turn, she then seeks
Her own following to coach, to teach.

Misleading storm rider, it really is
Mainly to herself she sings
Her many thought-inflated things,
Weighted with her special meanings.

But who am I to relate this so,
As I sought something perhaps to know,
Some wisdom through a will to grow,
When meeting her two weeks ago.

VI

CHANGES

Changes: Uninvited Guests

They arrived suddenly—
The day before, nothing, and then
There they were,
Bags packed to the fullest
Right under my eyes.

Oh, they'll leave soon, I thought,
Like other irritations—
But no, they stayed,
Settled in as if quite welcome,
These two visitors.

Delivered by my sinuses,
They require me to play
The gracious host,
And act as if this owlish look
Somehow is becoming.

Pruning

Over decades my way with surface surfaces.
Grounded more, I find a need to reveal more
Ground to contrast with the changes that my
Bright blooms bring, with repetition enough
In a picture of casual truths to seize some
Sort of beauty that appeals at least to me.

When a plant, or encroaching time, threatens
To overwhelm, to mask the ground,
Though it may be healthy in itself, maybe
Pruning can reshape it. If I cut it back,
Or even out, with care I can provoke
New growth, rebalance and restore.

With weeds, natives which elsewhere
Might be useful, even lovely, if contained,
Placement and judicious editing become essential.
Though I trim dead, unhealthy or merely
Undesired parts, I know that such severing
Can be too easy and ultimately radical.

Nature may abhor technology but speak too subtly
To me while I consider landscaping earthy things
Or my aging face. How much should remain ground
And how much covered to enhance, to shelter it?
What tools to use, if any? And how keep contrast,
Interest and change, while still maintaining grace?

Vain Lament

Now in the mirror still I see
The me that has to show itself,
And then I smile in mouth and eye—
Better so, but just adequate.

Now join, as predicted,
Those owlish bags, that packed,
Years ago stayed to my dismay
To guest a softening face,

And trembles below a jowly
Chin and newly hangs some neck
To emphasize each shake of head.
Now pride must leave that goes
Before such a seasoned fall.

We dare not speak of the rest of it—
Shoes that bind, pants which do not fit,
Nor the heaviness that shoulders
Bear despite a lowering chest.

Now would that wisdom have its day—
That quality said to increase with age,
But, if occasionally glimpsed,
In actuality, seems weaker too
And does not deign to stay.

Not in Time

The radio this morning revealed that
Multiple myeloma no longer kills in 95%
of cases, no longer means just two years to live
with pain and sudden snaps of bone

Now there are pills that can lead
to remission and a life, until something else
kills you first, and what's more—in a few years
there should be a cure

No more two hour weekly office waits
reached by labored walks on crutches
No more slow drip of chemotherapy
nor quiet taxing burn of radiation,
emergency hospital stays, shots, painful tests,
a chart for all those pills

What news— though I didn't hear it
when first it became fact seven years ago
then seven years after your death

So I wonder what time really heals
as news and experiences accumulate,
as on life's chalkboard, time and memory
smudge still more

Leaf Taking

In this harvest season when summer leaves
Leaves must fall and fall full on they do:
Sere flakes— serious now— clad
In crimson, in luminous orange
And yellow, ochre and rusted brown;
Wind takes them now— these leaves in thrall—
Harnesses them for one last whirl.

It is as if they ripened just for this—
This their final flowery flare—
As if dressing up for this dance to death.

Then bright too at first and soft
The cold that coldly comes
Escorting snow in silent steady dance.
But wind can whistle through bared branch
And armed as blizzard whitely blow
Mightily swirling stick and snow
Before quieting once again

To then allow the grounded snow to hold
And insulate, if what seeds remain below
Have strength and patience just to wait.

A Wife's Story, from PBS

My husband spanks his feet,
Believes them children—teenagers?
Each morning he wakes to me,
A stranger. His mirror holds an enemy.

Plaque, someone explains,
Are protein filaments in the brain;
He'll likely live for decades
But spend them in a slow decline.

Our daily life, she continues,
Is like a surgeon's claim:
His openings are large but each cut
Is small to minimize the pain.

It was to her husband's insight
And his humor that she was drawn,
But he no longer sees connection.
So much, she concludes, is gone.

Sport

There it goes again, racing round the bend
where I cannot see, but running, I follow
fast as possible— distracted by the thought
of tennis: seeing the ball and sending it

well, it's conditioning I think—
and speeding on, I reach the corner,
see the distant runner on the path
now become more even, and gaining just

enough, I pull out the name that fleeting
memory has hidden from me once again,
trying not to mark the time it's taken
but the triumph in the win.

Subtexts for Aging Female Football Fans

We sit, watching men collide
And gallop extravagantly, seeing
What they know of two-poled dreams
Of conquest by yard and strength.

Our younger selves, uninitiated
In this sport, viewed it in tones
Of black and white, saw then
A kaleidoscope of uniforms,
Clustering, patterning, and
Often leaving lumps on fields.

Now, colored by our informed years,
We see purpose in timed sailings
Of the missiled ball, in brief
Effective blocks and hits, the
Art in swiveling carries.
Such scripts seduce on battled fields.

A Crime

As the string pulled tighter
she leaned ever forward,
until at last no more give remained,
and her neck, steeled though it was,
snapped woodenly.

Ill-used far too often
and rarely clear-spoken,
her playing days are over;
she lies inert,
exposed and broken.

Finally an object only,
her graceful curves
curiously intact,
she is cruelly tagged
and always has been.

There is no question now
whether she will be other
than what she has become:
a useless guitar
abruptly past her prime.

Queries

When did you decide?
Was the slippery serpent an excuse?
Did it take days to suggest it?
Were you not busy enough?
Did you feel something missing?
Was it all too easy?
Did you wonder what would happen?
What it would be like after?

Eve adjusted her skirt slightly,
Smiled, and replied:
Yes.

Old Cypress Speaks

I stand bold amid rocks my roots have worried apart,
My remaining limbs reaching skyward. I am old, old, old.
Weathering has worn me to my core, in a thorough winnowing.
My roots still run deep, hidden and essential.
My outlook is dry, my look spare. Lit here on one side,
My bark skin long since shed, my woody veins are limned,
Echoing a craggy contour.

I reach out and out, limbs attenuated and pointed.
It is important, this sharpness, this definition: I am more
Myself than ever, defined in grays against a shaded sky.
The artist, gone to dust, has immortalized me, and I, him.
Do these darks and lights speak to you? My defined shape?
Oh, what lives I've seen, what's already been. Long past
Leaves or seeds, I hold this ground.

VII

VIEWPOINTS

Viewpoints

Beyond a narrow window, a broad tree trunk,
Limed in lichen, stands crisp against a whitish sky.
Wider windows frame flickering leaner stems,
Hardly separate with increasing rims of snow.
Do certain panes encourage growth?

Cole at two leans heavily on a high-handled truck,
Zigzagging fast across the floor; legs and walls
Block his way. If he can't maneuver, he does
Not wait to bump before he sounds a moaning wail.
Do obstacles move toward him?

A head cold makes me Alice-like of a sudden large,
And this room, which seemed so high in its ceiling
Rise to ridge, has become miniaturized to me.
You were little too, Max says, *until you grew*, implying
But still checking, Will I too?

I grin and nod. Almost four, he speaks of *edge* and *fragile*,
Describes oases in detail. Yet I worry about his pause
In jigsaw-working, recall saying, *This isn't coming together*,
While in front of him his puzzle part was still expanding.
Did my moaning quench his interest?

Later, Quincy at four waits in front of the fireplace
And requests, *When the fire gets big, can you call my name?*
As flames leap he asks his father, *Why can't you take wood
Off the house to burn?* Dad clarifies, *CHOP UP THE HOUSE?*
Q smiles, answers, *Just kidding*.

Mine!

Mine!
the two-year-old cries
     having just learned exclusivity
         possession entitlement
     proclaiming his selfhood

                Never again
will he be so sure
     so unchallenged

                Never again
will he own so much
be so small
     so full of promise

In the Moment

She took off her coat
And everything stopped,
As does he in his telling,
Looking around at us.

He resumes,
She was wearing a tie!
It seems his second grade love
Is fashion forward.

A Day of Swimming AND GEOCACHING

That way, Grandma, through the tunnel

    THROUGH FLOWERY FIELDS THAT BORDER BOG

I pull you at age two, you laughing Max-wise

    WE HOME IN WITH GPS COORDINATES

Again, just under the diving board

    HANDS TESTING TREE CAVES

Where you show me floating seeds

    WE WONDER, WHAT DOESN'T BELONG, AS WE TRAMP

That way, you say, *Again!*

    OVER WET STUMPS AND OTHER GOOD PLACES

Grandma swims you bubbling

    SHE CAN'T FIND ANY GEOCACHES

Pushing the boat of you

    BUT IT'S A GOOD DAY TO RETURN TO

You in blue-hued friendly water

Crane, Plow and Car Hope

These woods by Easy Street are safe,
though those nearby are likely not.
We serve our trees and vines,
And resting, rusting here, we use the air

as it uses us. Fire would be worse:
such speed would work a thorough
leveling to expose us all,
even those who leave us here

as the decades pass. Some, though,
find the beauty in us still:
our reddish oranges, mellowed browns,
our decaying, oddly thinning shapes.

The one who cuts the trees, his
saw loud and echoing, echoing:
he dare not risk exposure either.
Maybe we and our woods are safe.

Earthquake

Imagine the very earth moving,
Ground that until a few seconds ago
And the rest of your life before,
Supported you and now has become
Your enemy

Contemplate lying wedged
And half-blind for days like nights,
Knowing that you must wait,
Ready for just that single possible
Moment of discovery

Fall, 2001

A falling season,
This, as wind-borne
Leavings bare arboreal
And metal towers;
This fall delivers
A bold re-seasoning of us all.

Of all seasons, fall informs
Of future icy outrage.
Now fires of anger
Pierce indifference,
Cozy heat nonsensed,
In this all too righteous age.

Even reasoned measures
Take to caves; is this
Where the falling goes?
This fall we seem to know
Our gods, our might; may not
This mark an endless fall of night.

Language Lessons

Leaders orate to confound
Conflict comes as if we've had no hand
Crashing becomes hard landing
Peacekeeper missiles neutralize

Clear bunkers is to sanitize
Translate/conjugate: we/they kill
And having named the other evil
War becomes Goddamn simple

What is it about fire and light
Perhaps some ancestral seed
Pulsing warmth and a need
For vivid blood its sudden spurt

Red splashes and bursts of white
It's simple to connect these bits
These Rorschachs of vitality
Exciting and God forbid even lovely

Add holidays of explosive noise
Humanity seduced by science
Though sirens mimic wails of pain
Danger entices again and again

Torture

Many are the deadly
Tortures we invent:
A noose, the guillotine,
Feet in cement,
Hands/ arms wrapped up behind,
Body separated from mind,

Nails pulled, parts shocked,
Identity maimed and taken,
Faith and spirit knowingly shaken,
Young brains and bodies battered,
Bruised and distorted,
Soft and hardened bodies used,

Humans knifed, shot or drugged,
Flesh seared or branded.
In what/ whose name?
Who of us, what is to blame?
What ideas, wrongs, are of such might
That these inventions make them right?

Spring Politics

In this impatient time, throw mud words and forget
The raking; you might as well fabricate from half-cloth.
Dig it up, bury it; it's all the same when
Only point of view resists and governs.

Hot designer words fill the air as Orwell gravely sighs.
Until our final purchase of the farm, we are marketed
To by all, carefully convinced by minimal
Evidence directed through our fertile senses.

Any something heard again, again, again, and even
Known untruth gives up its *un*; lies lie fallow to later sprout.
Almost every Each seeks an Us, making You an Other.
Meanwhile, a moderate middle, disheartened, sinks.

On the President and His Intern

It's not prudishness, not delicacy,
that makes you so intense
about issues I'd rather not discuss.
Lying, I admit, is wicked,
though lord-knows we all do it.

In fidelity too we profess belief.
No, the point is of a moral system:
yours, of longer standing and
based on higher law, paternal,
absolute; your higher ground

advantageous. Yet in this case
I see you as self-righteous,
dictatorial, and impractical.
My view better suits the age:
flexible, relative, more cynical.

But then, amidst our prosperity,
such preaching against immorality
I can disregard; he's not,
thank-the-lord, my husband
and she is not my daughter.

Writing in 2009

Once begun, writing could go anywhere,
From a glimpse of sun beyond a tree,
A plot or path scarcely seen,
To an endearment or a lie.

Are you angry when a *decider* dithers,
Says he inherited what instead he leaves,
Labels a Mideast election as a coup,
And does not own up to his mistakes?

Is this now a fabled bottom
When most abjectly cash in chips,
As if markets were a game, greed
Simply strategy and shelter mere commodity?

A Cautionary Tale

Froggy Freddy would not jump,
Informed his parents he would not.
They asked, then begged, One little hop?
Even appealed to his artistic side:
Look, all others, when they jump, see colors
Streak across the sky. He shook his head.
They said, You must be fit; you must eat.
No, was all he would repeat.

Fall, and Freddy is now Fred.
Thin and determined, he stays and stays,
And others start admiring his ways.
Some even join him, but always say
They must go somewhere; he goes without.
Yes, this staid frog stands his ground.
Soon his words would gather meaning,
And others, listening, become eager
To join a movement, to call him leader.

Fred becomes Fredder, after his tendency
To name them all: giving them nicknames
Made them special, this they knew,
Helped his few words to them ring true,
And who could resist his personality,
His wisdom and his froggy grin.
So if at times he would not speak,
They asked and answered what he would say:
Even smarter, they thought, that way.

He became ever more widely known,
And Fredder knows best, often was said
Of him, the frog who stayed and stayed.
His legend grew, as he was left behind:
He was The Great One, known to all frogkind.

Worries

This was a restless night begun early
Amid mad mid-March weather,
When politicians impolitely pander
Here and there, day and night.

One self-styled chameleon
Markets many noxious thoughts,
Repeats and repeats his simple words,
To sway the angriest among us.

It was a restless night begun early;
Light jostles mind and signals change
Hinting of spring's reawakening
And of hope to combat daily fears.

My thoughts stick on a giant oak
That guards and dominates at the road;
Yesterday crane and chipper lingered there.
It still stands, will yield its crops

And shed more branches culled by wind
To take their berths in wetland wilds
Where restless predators and prey
Multiply and diminish in their turn.

We even worry for lack of worry
Here far from famine, bombs and bullets:
Something this way must be coming;
Build a bunker, hide the silver.

Forgiveness?

Is forgiveness
Denial
Of deeds wiped as if lives not lived
And generations of none
And mortal agonies
Did not exist?

Is forgiveness
Palimpsest
Substituting for memory
And enabling future sins?

Is forgiveness
Therapy
For even the distant ones
Who may bear scars that fade?

VIII

ART

Art: A Small Validation

Oh look, she's an artist,
The boy said of me
As I sat by an exquisite rose
Putting mere lines to paper
While my voices criticized.

He could not see my puny
Production, what tedious
Effort, the tentative
Wanderings accumulating
Beneath my cobwebbed pen.

Oh look, she's an artist,
The boy had said then.
Perhaps I'll remember him
So that he'll serve to joust
With my days and nights of doubt.

Stein Sits for Picasso

A Stein is a Stein
Is a Gertrude is
A true Stein is true
Is true is Gertrude Stein
And time for Stein is time
Is Stein is time for two
Four time to time for true
To time for Gertrude to be true

She sits it is true Stein sitting solid
She sits Stein sits seated for Picasso Stein sits
For she is seated it is true she sits true it is Stein
Picasso paints seated solid Stein sits seated true

A true Stein is there not there says Toklas not Stein

Toklas is not there is not Stein it is true Stein Picasso says it
Will be Stein it is true Stein Picasso paints Stein seated it is Stein

Ms Hesketh's Reading

The poet sat before us,
Delicate, pink and white,
Her voice soft and sharp,
And said, *If you're a reader—*
Defining and elevating us all—
Then you write by example.

She began writing at age ten,
Expanding on reading pieces
Of her varied work, and we
Wished but couldn't say
Since she appeared wan,
That she'd go on and on.

She ended by looking at us all
Before signing copies of her books
Suggesting, asking—
Some of you must write.
A gifted poet sat nearby
And unlike me quietly smiled.

Pantoum

This now will never come again
Never the same it can't be caught
Time is an abstract thing
As it carries us heedlessly along

Never the same it can't be caught
This precious thing that's not a thing
As it carries us heedlessly along
In a hurry to arrive elsewhere

This precious thing that's not a thing
Means more and more as we gather it
In a hurry to arrive elsewhere
We hasten to our lasting place

Used

My volume of <u>Dear Ghosts</u> is marked "used," but to what?
Ill- or well-? Beneath the title it is signed by Ms Gallagher,
"For Martha," to whose book the poet declares in scrawl
She is "looking forward."

Probably there are many such books, either written, to be
Written, or only dreamt of, referred to in such dedications,
But why did this evident admirer not keep the book?
What catastrophe overtook her or it?

Was it due to competing shelf space, a marketing decision?
Or was it a move, an illness, a death, a so-called life event?
Or was the slim tome forgotten, to be nearly discarded?
So radical, to give away a book,

Especially one so bright and new, which begins ironically:
"My Unopened Life/ lay to the right of my plate/
Like a spoon squiring a knife." The poem opens more
With each reading,

As it moves at first through darkness, the "shadowy penumbra
Of the madrona," below to worm, "acrobat of darkness," then
Into the belly of the bird. The spoon ricochets between bowl
And "cave" of mouth and is left,

As is the room, as is the poet. This one poem can be used,
Repeatedly opened, to prize open life and memory, as subtly
It spoons darkness to light and back, reverberates, and
Spoons spirit into loss.

THE WOULD-BE SCULPTOR EYES
THE FOLLY OF PERFECTION

So easy to feed even summer's fire
The well-intentioned wooden piece,
Its wily surface attacked by days
Of hours in effort still too weak.

Too easy to miss-estimate: cut a limb
More useful than imagined; slide
From any perch; comment a step too far;
Overburden a heavy foot or heart.

How foolish to crave what came before
The uncut wood or ripening seed,
To seek the unvarnished ring of truth,
Clarity of thought or memory.

Compare sky's drift of landscape
To the vacuous mist seen from above.
Discard that what we get is what we see;
Imagine, create and then just be.

Oh, See

OCD, this obsessive compulsion is called:
Impulse once felt that cannot be denied.
A fix seems simple: leave one thing awry,
But one in number is appallingly worse,
Because, like anything singly misaligned,
One stands out, jumps up, virtually shouts,
Straighten me, tighten me, make me right!

No, nor two things done, so better three,
For three is magic, simpler than five or seven.
Three doesn't demand two's exactitude
Of right and left, upright and even;
Each two must match in numerous ways.
Three, however, is a group, which then
Becomes a form that too must fit its space.

Like time, such work can expand
Or even contract in a rush.
A rule can measure time or place,
And tick of each to ever smaller piece,
Until one cannot hold or even see a bit.
To attempt this one tries far too hard,
And precision is then all and none of it.

Pleas

Ed(d)i, tall and very strong,
many-limbed and long of arm,
takes care of business as if it's hers,
thinks she's more useful than she is.

We both, that is, the I that's me,
are subject to her whys and wheres,
for whom and when, will what be done.

Oh Ms Tor, please wait your turn,
earn a place, save your scorn,
or else each thing you long to rule
will be aborted or worse, still-born.

Now hold on, this other warns,
you use me for what is or may go wrong;
it's not my fault I've grown so strong.

So in the name of good psychology,
let's respect our roles and get along:
a tri-part me, an all in one,
to enjoy the doing and the done.

Blocked?

I could write, you know. Sure, I could
Write about a woman who could write.
Easier to write about one who couldn't;
I could sit here and do nothing.

A Woman on the Verge—now that's
A good title. A bit derivative, but what isn't.
Verge, virgin, version: verge of what
You ask, and well you might.

She would maybe start to move,
This woman, start to talk, maybe start
To live, or think about starting.
Or just start to think, how about that.

Maybe there's a sound and so
Then she starts, as in startle,
Like a wind-up toy,
Not quite wound down.

There, almost nothing, and then
Something. What no one understands,
Something from nothing. Do we have
To be there for it to be?

Where are we in the scheme of things?
An evil plot, or clever? Schemer,
What a name for an almighty.
But enough little questions.

Back to this woman, there where she
Sits, stands, stares, starts, with us here,
Looking, wondering, wandering.
And I did write, didn't I.

Transition: ESL Exercise

For many *generations*
Vespers was a time of prayer
And quiet contemplation.

Dusk on the wide river
Brought a certain measure
Of *serenity*: water quieted,

And whatever *cargo* the barge
Hauled seemed to lie lighter
On its *scarred* surface.

Above, the *helter-skelter*
Splarge of stars slowly brightened,
Forming a *lintel* of sorts

Over the floating folk,
In whose *retentive* eyes
Points of light danced and sparkled.

Thus whatever *maleficent* forces
There were in the universe,
They were not *apparent*

Here, in this location, in these
Moments, as night approached
And *raucous* day receded.

If I Were Famous

There would be applause before I did anything,
and likenesses of my face would grace many publications.
There would be stoppings on streets, greetings in restaurants;
hangers on would wait for each word, hungry for morsels of my truths.
Reporters would rush to my door, make it a familiar place;
areas would need to be cordoned off.

I would accumulate layers of print; myths would develop.
Where I went, when, and with whom would become fodder
for the press and even my head peering out to check the weather
would become a photo op.

My mysteries would become public and inventions abound.
I'd become infinitely interesting and wouldn't need to leave my house,
but when I did the lines would part and awed murmurs would ripple
through the crowds, susurrus of: *there she is; she looks so good, just
like her pictures; that's her, Mommy, lift me up; that's who I want to be.*

My patient driver would stand by while I signed my latest best-seller;
fans would proffer pens and treasure those I'd touched, tell me
that I changed their lives, weep for joy.

Oprah, Diane and Katie would interview me, and Barbara Walters
couldn't make me cry. I would be witty for hours, knowing instinctively
which camera afforded viewers my best side.

I'd look for ways to use my dollars, far too much for me and my large
family. Trim and brilliant fifty-year-old men—no, 45 and younger—
would be besotted.

Piles of journals, mountains of my work, would be sorted and snatched at; editors would come to me, return my words in perfect form; I could nod and smile—*exactly right, what I meant*, my encouragement all that's needed for further work to be hurried into print.

I'd have to choose between invitations, fit in one event after another, but take care not to tire of incessant visits to the White House and the Vatican. My jet's understated design would be seen on HGTV, and I'd have so many guards that my homes would remain private, with photo shoots allowed only two days a week on just the public floors.

I would choose which libraries and museums could acquire my work; my accountants would suggest which pieces and for how much, even as dealers violently bid up others.

Work would flow from my fingers, pen and brush mere extensions for my endless perfection. My new words would outnumber Shakespeare's, my proficiency overshadow his. Leonardo's name would come second, as my notebooks filled with sketches for devices as yet undreamed of by others; future generations would gasp— *how could she have known?*

And when I died, my body would rest in state, preserved behind glass, and mourners would mean it when they said how good I looked, and it would be true, that lying there, just that way— a national treasure, I'd never looked better.

Dark Musings

In the early lightness of night
It is not and is a challenge
To see that which you cannot
And fathom in part within
The watery business of the back
What might be there

Back in the thinning thick
Where woodpeckers knock beak on bark
Of hollowing over-watered trees
Still standing in this pre-winter winter
As we wonder which trials
Will be lived or not

Which little extinguishments
Will be there or here
Where tree-falls are plentiful
With or without sound
As if it matters really
If we are here to hear or not

Silent Sunlight

Silent sunlight speaks
In streaks of steamy color.
Shade is banished by her voice.

Silent sunlight screams exposure,
Evokes all colors,
No one better than another.

Silent sunlight speaks
Her daily show and tell.
Sleep is not for her,
Subtlety not her subject.

Silent sunlight sets the stage,
Grows the scenery,
Fuels the drama.
See, she proclaims,
Summoning for us our world.

Impossible, That

I held the world for an instant
And it was light
And all my worries went rushing by
Like the wind

And I heard sighs, screams, laughter and song:
The sound of billions
In the silence of that second.